ENDLESS

SHORE

Published By

POETRY WORLD ORG

Copyright © POETRY WORLD ORG 2020

First Edition : 2020

ENDLESS SHORE

Editor

Pakeeza Rizvi

Special Credits

Dr.Niveditha

Nitin Chopra

Johannes Kraisler

Sheetal Yadav

Mahi R.V

INDEX

ALISHA ADHANA

Alisha Adhana,

a lawyer by profession and a writer at heart.

It was back in 2017 when she got her first book published

titled

"Queendom Of Dreams"

That book had both her heart and soul where she expressed

19 poems, encapsulating the young spirit of the young

hearts.

She vows to further cherish every sentiment that the heart

beholds and flick a flare of emotions.

THE WHINING THUNDERBOLT

Never knew it was just about the skin,

Which you treated just like a bin.

For me, it was about pure love,

And you pounced upon with a lustful tub.

Why was I just another option for you?

I believe you were just full of pitch dark hue.

Whenever your skin touched mine, it felt so fine,

But it was hard to believe that this story was just about, Painful whine.

I drank a flagon of anguish,

To make through this wreathing torment,

Is my last wish.

THE REBUFF ENDEARMENT

The day we met caused utter friction,

But how would I know it was for a future rejection?

Your words were just another lullaby,

But I wonder they were said just for another bye.

My heart pounded for mere words of appreciation,

Oh! My love! Then why am I now leading a life
of deprivation?

My wonder world just came to an end,

When I realized you forgot the gala moments

we did spend.

ONE LAST LOVE

It was an end to a beautiful path,

Yes, it was my last love from finish to start.

There have been tales brewing first love,

I wonder how tormenting was my last love.

Silly, were those days of feeling just happy as a kid,

Well, making things worse was all he did.

There was a time when the heart pumped with love

and blush,

What brutal days turned this repository pale and

sacred love to flush.

Still crave for that one last hug,

Yes, this is nothing but that one last love.

THE BURNING SENSATION

All I did was to trust,

But my spirit was given a deep thrust.

Every night the soul drips in pain,

The enchanting efforts just all went in vain.

Feelings were indeed a quintessence,

But they played with my heart and created nuisance.

All is left now, the chips and bits of a broken heart,

Oh! I hope an angel drops in to carry this torment

in a joyful cart.

WHAT I AM IS A MYSTERY

What I am is a mystery,

To what I was is a history.

As the years passed by,

The spirit in me got crumbled to fly.

I was a breeze of fresh air,

But the world toppled, and nothing stands fair.

The shattered bits find their way back,

That was long lost over the lusty track.

The heart ponders upon old rock love,

It awaits the presence of a tender dove.

THE UNSPOKEN

Some feelings are not to be spoken,

Rather be felt or it leaves the heart, broken.

Wonder what the chapters in my life taught?

Just when I rewind the play,

it's some food for thought.

Amidst all the ups and downs,

Some got healed and some were brutal wounds.

What they have given me is regret for life.

Why it was so easy for them rather

I always had to fight?

Maybe the battle still goes on.

There still lies a dilemma; who is a lover,

who is a foe.

One day all this will have a beautiful end,

There won't be a disparity between a lover

and a friend.

THE ABANDONED WARMTH

Profoundly I opened my heart,

All you did was hit it with a spiking dart.

How merry would have been the future?

If you protected my heart and been its

endearing tutor.

There is too much to run through the

paleness of past,

As we both knew, there were memories too vast.

All you did was to strip my soul apart,

But for me, to keep you guarded was my art.

THE TWO SOULS

You were a soothing breeze to my heart
Just like how cherry tops the tart.

How can I forget the day I met you?
It was just like an Ocean with a wonderful view.

The chills of our souls entangled
Was nothing less than something perfectly angled.

The spark of kissing your soul is profound
All I wish is to keep you around.

The heart craves you just like wine
May two perfect souls be together for a lifetime.

SURVIVAL

The soul wanders for survival
But society is its biggest rival.

The wounds life gave were so grave
All dreams that popped were flushed in a wave.

The heart ponders for a sigh of hope
Wonder, will ever the mind be out of dope.

Long gone are those days of love and joy
The clock is ticking! Work, hustle, rush ohh boy!

God gave us the gift of life
And here we fight the battle to survive.

All we need is a lorry to travel in time
So that we breathe fresh and super fine.

Yet, the soul wanders for survival
And still the society be its biggest rival.

AMAN PRASAD SHAW &

SURYA CHAKRABORTY

Aman Prasad Shaw and Surya Chakraborty,

boys from a middle class family of West Bengal,

Kolkata have a God gifted feature to reach people as writers

of short stories, poems and quotes. Surya from 20th

August 2000 and Aman from 27th March 2000, started

their life and at the age of 19 years they worked as co-

authors of many books such as Mystical Musing, Era of Love

etc. and besides that they work as the

authors of LOVE LIFE.

LOVE LIFE is their own solo book which covers the best poems and quotes. Besides this they are also active in social media such as Instagram and Facebook where anyone can follow them back.

Instagran ID: aman_2718 and cheifsurya007.

Facebook ID: Aman Prasad Shaw (Mr Perfect) and Surya Chakraborty.

NO RAPE

Uche darje me bithao,

Unhe samman dilao,

Gande najro ko na chalao,

Gandegi ko hatao.

Shaktiyo ke rupo me birajti hai wo,

Maa bankar tumko dharti pe lai hai jo,

Har dushmano se tumhe bachati rahe wo kyu,

Taki bada hokar tum aise jallal ban sako.

Jo tumhe palte unhi par tum apne nazar hai

gandi dalte,

Maa bahen tumhari bhi hai ye kese bhul jate ho

tum,

Raste me chalte ladkiyo ko kyu aise cherte tum,

Insan hai woh koi janwar nahi,

Jinda jala dete ho, kya tumme koi insaniyat hai

ki nahi,

Socho kabhi tumhare maa pe koi aise war kiya
hota,
Tab iss duniya me tumhara astitwoh kaha hota,
Aaj na he tum rehete na he gande kamo me
ulajte,
Apne appko aise jalal bana ke ,
Hawas ka nanga nach dikhake,
Khudko janwar banake kya mila,
Jara socho jara socho dhayan se kya mila,
Aise gandagi ko hamare samaj se hatao,
Aise janwar ko fansi me jhulao ya golio se urao,
Samaj se hatao surakshit rasto ko banao,
Aise he chalte raha toh jaldi desh dub jayega,
Piche ke taraf se phela sthan me rahega,
Aise mombattiya jala kar kuch bhi na ho payega,
Sirf danda he sahara hai jisse unhe sudhara
jayega,

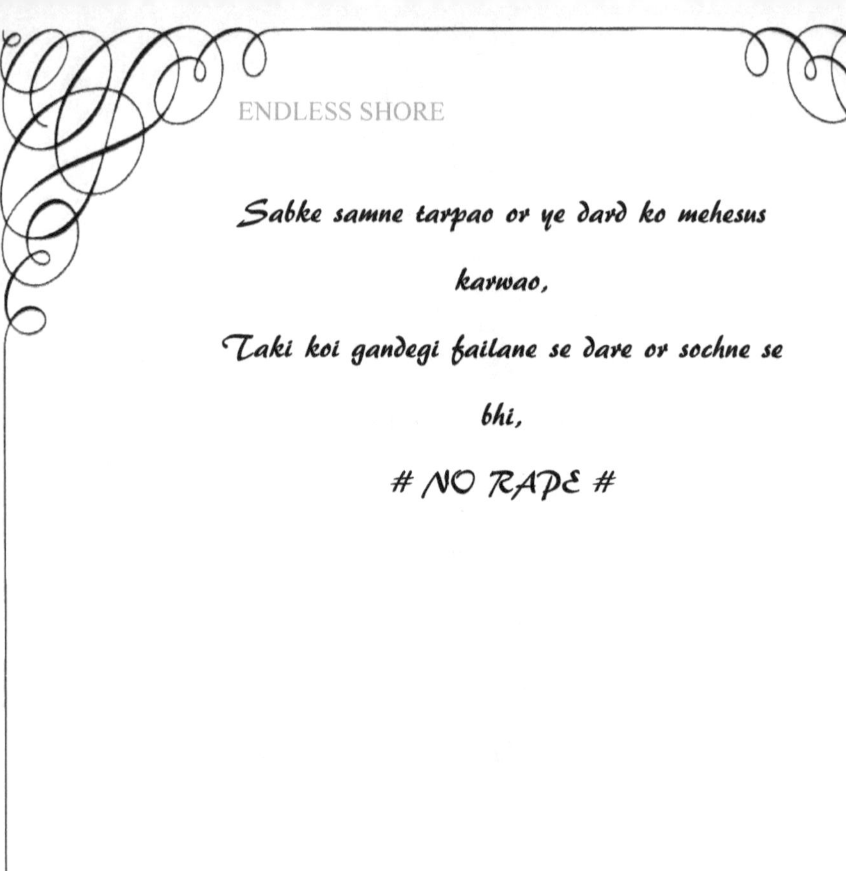

Sabke samne tarpao or ye dard ko mehesus

karwao,

Taki koi gandegi failane se dare or sochne se

bhi,

 # NO RAPE #

BACHPAN

Sacchi hasi lauta sakte ho kya?

Suno waqt bachpan laa sakte ho kya?

Cheen ke ye mobile

Mujhe mera khilona lauta sakte ho kya?

Suno waqt thora piche jaa sakte ho kya?

Nahi chahiye ye azadi wali zindagi

Wo maa ki god ki kaid dila sakte ho kya?

Suno waqt wo bhai se bachpan wali ladai lauta

sakte ho kya?

Ye gaadi, waadi to theak hai

Wo meri 3 pahiyo wali cycle laa sakte ho kya

Suno waqt phir se girna seekha sakte ho kya?

Ab logo ke liye has ke thak chuka hoon

Meri aapni hasi lauta sakte ho kya

Suno waqt, phir se waise hasna seekha sakte ho

kya?

Jhuti hasi chehre pe, akele me chupke rone se

thak gaye hai

Sabke samne rone ki azadi dila sakte ho kya

Suno waqt, maa ki aanchal lauta sakte ho kya?

Ye plan karke, milane ke liye restaurant decide

karne wale dost to hai

Par kya wo sadak pe ek sath daurane wale dosto

se milwa sakte ho kya

Suno waqt, bachpan lauta sakte ho kya?

ZINDAGI KE DO RASTE

Har kisiko pana hamara naseeb nahi hota,

Sitaaro ko ginne ke chakkar me aksar log

chand ko hai khota,

Yaado me kaid karke rakhne se agar,

Uss insan ko paa lena mumkin hota to,

Sirf yaado ko sath lekar koi bhi na rota,

Jise kho diya use wapis pana har kisi ka

kismat nahi hota

Kahi laakho me ek do mil jaye karte hai,

Qki dil se pasand aane wala har insaan

uske liye sahi nahi hota,

Magar in sab baato ko sochkar dil ko,

Kisi or se pyar mohabbat bhi to nahi hota.

Zindagi hamesha do raste diya karte hai,

Jaha hume sochne parte hai ki hume

kisme chalne hai,

Ek pyar mohabaat ke hote hai to dusre

zindagi ke sawal hote hai,

Galat raste chunne par aakhir pachtana

hume he parta hai,

Yaha zindagi kisiko koi dusra moka nahi

deta,

Jo safalta ke raste pe chalte hai usko,

Pyar nibhane wala nahi milte

Ye ajib khel hai zindagi ka,

Jaha pyar or safalta dono ek saath sabko

naseeb nahi hota...

****

Koi khushiyon ki chaaha mein roya

Koi dukho ki panaah mein roya,

Ajeeb silsila hai ye zindagi ka...

Koi bharose ke liye roya

Toh koi bharosa karke roya...

Kaash meri zindagi me aaye

Ek aise barsaat,

Mere hath mein ho tera haat,

Bheegte rahe hum saari raat,

Honth rahe khamosh

Bas aankhon se ho teri meri baat...

Kadwahat bhare iss daur mai

Jubaan par apne mithaas

Rakhte hain,

Rote bhi hai alag andaaz main,

Chehre pe muskaan barkarar

Rakhte hain...

*****

Kuch pal zindagi ke

Itne khaas hote hai

Wo shakhs yadd rahe ya na rahe

Par unke sang guzare lamhe har pal

Yadd rehte hai...

Samundar na ho toh, Kashti kis kamm ki?

Mazzak na ho to, Masti kis kamm ki?

Doston ke liye qurban hain ye zindagi...

Agar dost na ho to phir zindagi kis kamm ki...

******

Tumhe barish pasand hai,

Mujhe baarish me tum

Tumhe hasna pasand hai,

Mujhe haste hue tum

Tumhe bolna pasand hai,

Mujhe bolte hue tum

Tumhe sab kuch pasand hai,

Aur mujhe bas tum...

ANAND KANAUJIYA

Anand Kanaujiya, an electrcal engineer by study and profession. He completed his M.tech in Electrical Engineering from IIT BHU Varanasi. Currently, residing in Lucknow - The city of Nawab's in Uttar Pradesh.

He has a great impact of kashi in his life and he started to play with the words at the bank of Holy Ganges. Basically he calls himself the engineer of words. He places them, combines them, tunes them to create a poetic compounding.

Basically he writes about love, romance, nature and relationship philosophy with a touch of spiritual connection.

The journey that started from kashi is still going on and he has published two books till date - Darpan And Hamsafar. He has also been a part of many anthologies like Axile of Thoughts, Aath Dham Assi. He also own two blogs by the name of ANUNAAD.

1. Anandkanaujiya.blogspot.com

2. Anunaadak.com

Facebook page - Anunaad.

OTHER BOOKS BY THIS AUTHOR

तुमसे प्रेम....कुछ यूँ भी!

लोग प्रेम के न जाने क्या क्या रूप लिखते हैं,
मैं तो तेरा नाम लिखता हूँ।

मैं खुश, बेहद खुश रहता हूँ क्यूँकि
साथ तेरे बिताए लम्हें मैं अपने संग लेकर चलता हूँ।

कुछ इस तरह हमने तुमको हमसफर बना लिया है,
ख्वाबों के सफर पर मैं हमेशा तेरे साथ चलता हूँ।

बातें बड़ी नही करता क्योंकि मैं झूठ नही बोलता
मैं तुझ पर दावा कि तुम मेरे हो, कभी किसी से नही करता हूँ।

जो पल दिए तूने वो आज भी क़ैद हैं दिल के तहख़ाने में,
रिहा नही करता इन्हें, मैं तेरे साथ का लालच आज भी रखता हूँ।

तेरा साथ ही आनन्द...

आपकी बातों में छुपी शैतानियाँ समझते हुए भी वो अनजान बनते हों...

जब समझाओ तो ज्यादा होशियार न बनो, ये कहकर बातों को टाल देते हों...

इससे ज्यादा कोई रिश्ता क्या मुकम्मल होगा, कि दोनों दिल एक ही मुकाम पर हैं...

तू बस उनके साथ सफ़र को जी, इससे ज्यादा की क्यों उम्मीद करते हो...

ज्ञान !

ज्ञान बहुत है सबके पास तुम्हें अब बहुत मिलेगा, तू लेता रह,
बुरे वक़्त में ऊँट पर बैठे बौने को भी लंगड़ी कुतिया काट
लेती है ।

सब्र रख और मुस्कुराकर लोगों के हाव भाव देख, ये नयी बात
नही,
जिन्हें कभी बोलना तुमने सिखाया था, उनकी भी बात सुननी
पड़ती है।

तूफ़ान है अभी दरिया में बहुत तेज, थम जा ज़रा,
मौसम साथ न दे तो नाव क़रीने से पार करनी पड़ती है।

दिन को सूरज यूँ ही नसीब नही होता, तुमको पता होगा,
उसे भी ये काली अंधेरी रात पूरी इंतज़ार में बितानी पड़ती है ।

इश्क़ बनारस ...

तुम्हारे सर पे पल्लू और बंद आँखो से नज़रें हटाना
मुश्किल है.......
तुम मिले भी तो बाबा के दरबार में जहां रुकना भी मुमकिन नही
होता।

सुनो, पीपे के पुल के शोर में कुछ भी सुन पाना बड़ा मुश्किल
है......
और बिना सगड़ो तुगको ताकना कि तुम्हारा बोलना बंद
नही होता ।

बनारस की नशीली हवाओं में सीधे खड़े रहना भी
मुश्किल है......
उस पर तुम्हारे हाथों से मिली ठंडई का क़हर कम नही होता ।

मिज़ाज अक्खड़ बनारसिया कि कदमों का ठहरना ज़रा मुश्किल
है.....
उस पर तुम्हारे सोलह सोमवार का व्रत का असर कम नही
होता ।

कुछ मुलाक़ातों बातों में कोई कहानी बनाना बड़ा
मुश्किल है......
इस तरह बिन बताए गोदौलिया की भीड़ में कोई साथ नही
छोड़ता।

अब तो यहाँ किनारों पर एक एक पल भी काटना
मुश्किल है......
ये वही अस्सी घाट ही है जहां दिन का भी पता नही चलता।

बीतती शाम के साथ दिल को सम्भालना बड़ा मुश्किल है......
अब तो गंगा आरती पर भी उनका आना जाना नही होता ।

अब तो गंगा किनारे यूँ ही तनहा भटकना भी मुश्किल हैं......
तुम्हारी यादों का कारवाँ कभी साथ ही नही छोड़ता।

मोहब्बत और तुम !

क्या ख़ाक असर होगा अल्फ़ाज़ों के समंदर में,
दिलों की बात समझने को आंखों के ये इशारे ही काफ़ी है....

तुमने कभी देखकर यूँ ही मुस्करा दिया था,
और हम आज तक तेरी मुस्कान का मतलब ढूँढ रहे हैं.....

उनको शिकायत है कि हम उन पर गौर नही करते !
गौर करने वाली बात है कि शिकायत भी हमसे ही......

तुम तो मेरे लिए यूँ ही बेवजह बेहद ख़ूबसूरत थे....
तुमको या दूसरों को मैं इसकी वजह क्या बताऊँ ?

ये जो मेरे हिस्से में रात सुहानी है....
तेरी ही तो निशानी है!

वो दुवाओं में भी अपना हुस्न बरकरार माँगती है ,
हमसे दीवानगी वो कुछ इस क़दर बयाँ करती है।

मदहोश करने को इन तरंगों में वेग कितना है....
मुझमें उठती है जो तेरी उँगलियों के छूने के अन्दाज़ से।

काश तुम भी इस बारिश सी होती
तुम बरसते और हम भीगते !
और ये सिलसिला यूँ ही चलता रहता...

सुना है बेमौसम बरसात भी होती है,
तुम भी मिल लिया करो.... कभी... बेवजह..../
बरस बीते, और अब तो तेरे दिए सभी घाव भी भर गए हैं...../
लेकिन कमबख़्त ये पुरवी बयार..... काफ़ी है.... तेरी याद दिलाने
को !

मैं बनारस !

जब हमने बनारस को छोड़ा था,

एक हिस्सा अपना वहीं छोड़ा था !

निकल पड़े थे निभाने दुनिया की रवायतों को,

शरीर साथ था मगर आत्मा को वहीं छोड़ा था।

पहले कुछ और ही आनंद था ये जानने वाले ये बताते हैं

हम भी पूछने वालों को अपनी कहनी कुछ यूँ सुनाते हैं ,

जन्म तो कहीं और ही हुवा था हमारा ये सब जानते हैं,

पर पुनर्जन्म का स्थान तो सबको हम बनारस बताते हैं   ।

किरदार क्या हूँ मैं, कैसे बयाँ करें तुमको, हम नही जानते हैं,

एक नाम मिला था आनन्द हमें और सब इसी से पहचानते हैं,

किसी ने पूछ लिया कि तुम्हारे बारे में कुछ और जानना चाहते हैं

बनारस के पहले या बाद? जीवन के यही दो हम अध्याय

बताते हैं।

सर्द इश्क़...

रंग कई रूप कई
रोज़ कोई कहानी नई।

दिन वही रात वही
ज़िंदगी वही तारीख़ नई।

शख़्स वही प्यार वही
कहाँ से दूँ दलीलें नई?

उन्नीस वही बीस वही
उन्नीस-बीस की बात नई।

गर्मी वही सर्दी वही
सर्द इश्क़ में गर्मी नई।

समय का ताना-बाना ...

मानवीय प्रकृति

अजीब सी!

स्मृतियों में उलझा

बुनता है भविष्य

वर्तमान में

और

खबर नही

वर्तमान की!

अंधी सियासत !

तुम मुझसे मेरे होने का सुबूत माँगते हो
तुम वही हो ना जो भूतों में यक़ीन रखता है .....!

अच्छे हैं जो आँख से अंधे हैं
मुझे तो अक़्ल के अंधों पर तरस आता है .....!

ख़ैर छोड़ो तुमको सुबूत क्या देना
जो अपनों का ना हुवा हमारा क्या होगा .....!

बहुत मुमकिन है कि तुमको तुम्हारी औक़ात याद दिला दें
मगर छोड़ो, तुमको समय देकर इतनी भी इज्जत क्यूँ दी जाए.....!

आज सितारे गर्दिश में सही मगर रोशनी बाक़ी है अभी
तुमको जला कर ख़ाक करने को एक चिंगारी ही काफ़ी होगी.....!

वक्त है अभी सम्भाल जाओ ऐ ऊँची उड़ान वालों
लौट कर हर परिंदे को ज़मीन पर ही आना है .....!

इतिहास और सियासत !

ये जो बड़े गर्व से अपना इतिहास सुनाते हैं, जरूर अमीर होंगे,

क्योंकि गरीबों का कोई भूत, भविष्य और वर्तमान नही होता।

भूखा पेट, प्यासे होठ और अधनंगे बदन वालों का कोई देश नही होता,

रोटी धर्म इनका और जाति गरीबी, इनके पास लड़ने को हिंदुस्तान पाकिस्तान नही होता।

वीरता और महानता के किस्से लिखे और पढ़े गए केवल राजाओं के,

युद्ध में लड़ने वाले सिपाहियों की बहादुरी के बताओ कितने किस्से सुने हैं तुमने?

तुम्हारा तो कोई इतिहास नही कोई नाम नही, बताओ कौन सुनेगा तुमको,

और वो जो ऊँचाई पर है, तुम पर तरस भी खा लें तो महान हो जाते हैं।

ये सियासी खेल है सियासत के बड़े-2 लोग इसे खेलते है,
तुम भी जरूरी हो इस खेल में वरना ये किसकी जिंदगी से खेलेंगे।

AVNI RATRA

Avni Ratra, a girl from Faridabad, pursuing Masters in Economics, has a deep connection with writing, a passion that ignited years ago has found its way and glory.

She is an introvert who pens her life as 'a worthy experience with aromatic memories and gestures that life comes with'.

She believes, a small and simple life goes inside her mind where she features her as a protagonist, playing her role with utmost ease and pleasure.

She finds poetry soulful, penning her thoughts makes her introspect self, it liberates and calms her mind. She is a profound lover of 'nature ' and finds joy in weaving her poems taking inspiration from the essentials of life.

Instagram id- theinkedenvelope

LUCKY THAT WE ARE HAPPY

PREFACE :

What it encloses is indeed very special, superficial and unique in every respect. There is every reason to recreate each minute detail set in the backdrop of the phase that emerged to be the defining era of friendship. The moments have accompanied us since the inception of our friendship, on the path of our lives to teach the lessons that life could ever impart. Friendship could be rejoicing and enticing, hardly could I understand, had I not met you. When life plans for you, it chooses a paradise for you, the loved ones, whom we nurture and preserve for our life, our earned credentials for life. Happiness is when they become a part of your identity and, you; reflect in them, through their actions, words or every breath witnesses the essence of acquaintance. We earned this friendship, a lot we owe to it.

Friendship is as pure and enriching as breathing freely, it reconnects mind to silence, silence for a deeper introspection of self, that's so real people grow in friendship. Friendship is experiencing highs and lows of life with your companions, it is the most basic relationship in life.

CHAPTER 1 : A SECOND CHANCE

It was a second chance, all that life could ever give. We were the innocent school companions, who had no idea as to what life had in store for us. I believe, great things happen by chance, and by choice, it becomes incredible, an indelible part of life. It takes no effort to be with you!

The anonymity was very vivid for long, the early stage of our life did not witness friendship. The school companions did not count on each other for anything, we had our comfort in the hands of others.

The two blossoming flowers were planted in the same soil, nurturing in the same environment inherited special values, a boundary kept them away. Hardly the innocent girls could interpret the boundary, continued to live at their own pace. But, life comes with millennial surprises, our union was a beginning to an enthralling experience. What came next was a series of ups and downs which became a testimony, an evident trial, and an auspicious bond.

Here it lies beauty in a second chance!

A chance becomes a beautiful and life-changing choice when two independent souls unite to explore each other's life in-depth and accept every scar to perceive a flawless human in each other's life. There is always a lot to say, but I choose to remain silent to let my eyes communicate the unsaid and let the warmth of love transcend into our life. So, every moment spent becomes a benchmark to reinstate the definition of friendship. A second chance, an infinitesimal beautiful choice!

Turn on to the new page, a new beginning of the second chance. You know, love is not, at first sight, it is a gradual comfort that one gets in an association. When I first met you I had no clue where this acquaintance would take us, I was unaware of its magic. But, it worked like a remedy for my life. It did wonders to believe that in life, friends are saviors and their presence makes life lit.

So the two strangers met one day and slowly they built their trust, stood firm by each other's side and made their definition of forever. Often a special character comes from the heart, here it is the heart that portrays a journey in the shape of characters, who have lived each part and made memories to be captured in words and recreate the visuals before them, as if it is childhood once again.

CHAPTER - 2 : OF ITS PART

Many miniature stories form a part of this incredibly fascinating story. Each one is symbolic of friendship, as the inner and the outer chords that make life symmetric and upright. Friends imbibe every emotion.

The two figures stood entirely apart from each other despite being placed in a very closed environment, there was a medium lacking to get them on board with each other. Things did not rush nor did they become used to each other's company. Nostalgia takes me right to the nodal point.

We saw each other daily,

the school going girls,

from the same origin,

to a similar destination.

We never shaked hands,

We never kept secrets of each other,

then,

I wonder why,

the vibes did not connect.

Then.

Oh, girl!

What took us so long to

comprehend our silence

into a never-ending conversation.

Above all,

How, When and Why

I got you at the right time

To be in my frame of happiness!

Undoubtedly, it was not easy to keep everything aligned or in proportion for the young girls. Their little minds had little perceptions about the idea of friendship, maybe what their previous friendship taught them to be. This one was quite different, it began on a very formal note. We were competitors before companions, a little proximity and a little less adaptability.

Back then, we were shuffled, like the ones migrating, displaced from their homeland seeking peace in a new place and format. The scenario changed, the culture was not involved for an introvert, I had my companions the next door. It was a strange land, I seemed lost as if it was day one. But, it had to happen one day.

It was the beginning 'Of Its Part!'

The Phase One...........

वो पहली बार था,

वो पहला phase था

देखा, मगर मिले नहीं,

फिर साथ थे, तो समझा नहीं।

जब समझे, तो समझ आया,

कि यह वही दोस्ती है

जो नजरों ने जानी थी,

बस दिल ने तब मानी नहीं।

A lot began from Phase One, our second chance proved a bliss, a fine minute of understanding in life, all that we could sense and interpret. The foundation of Phase Two...

Familiar with Family!

She was one family in this universe. I was on the other side, happily planting flowers in my garden. Soon, she bloomed my world, expanded my circle and accepted me her place. We made our friendship a new home, moving from familiarity to family. The boundary moved and we stepped in shaping the new relationship.

CHAPTER 3 : A NEW BEGINNING

It was gradual, a non altering acquaintance began in several moments we walked into the initial formal talk, among a group but stood apart, forming its beautiful world, fresh and crisp, memories being a testimony to the silent up and downs.

A journey began in silence, but the echo was loud in our ears. The echo of love reciprocated each time we poured in small efforts into creating an eventful journey. We were a finite structure independently, together we scaled a meter of infinity, celebrating with the colors of sky and rainbow.

It was new,

it was a fresh start.

A new slate,

fresh ink.

to engrave a new emotion

naturally into our blood,

it runs endlessly,

from the heart to heart,

Every sense

counting on the beauty,

of how it binds our life

in a thread.

A promise to eternity,

You and Me,

will be my finest frame.

Forever!

A Bright Colour!

Keen to be together, contented to be our self in each other's company, we grew. Similar but a pinch of contrast was a full-on blast in this pair, with a phase of learning by the mistakes to how mistakes keep the child in every heart young, we figured silence in sadness. Little madness added to the fun, like a cherry on the pie.

Hi, Miss,

Onboard with me, you covered Years. A second chance and a new beginning. A blank space, the new writers, the amateur artists, the patient teens, the curious adults, all and many more traits we had.

To the History, and to the forthcoming time, here is a small revival down the Memory Lane. Turning On..........

You Are !!

A toast,

to the vintage times,

to the warm memories,

that are my old school companions.

You are in the frame of happiness,

Of the days,

that planted sunflowers in

my garden of life.

Oh! ,

You pretty girl,

For how long have you been a shade

A soothing shade,

in my life.

How long have you been a constant

support,

to recover your loved ones from pains.

A person in you,

So pure that she knows to Love,

Love Eternally, unconditionally.

A deed is done years back,

to commit self with you

and your acquaintance,

Flipping the pages,

there is freshness

And a sight to behold in my eyes.

CHAPTER – 4 : A CLASSICAL TALE – WHEN AND HOW '2' IS ONE

Yes, 2 is one, certainly. It exists in friendship, as it comes naturally with the person whom you feel connected and self-liberated. The most credible title of any friendship is the magic that makes one self-liberating.

A pick from the classics, a handcrafted story of two young girls who walked in as strangers, walked out each other's confidant.

We were 11 or 12, when we formally greeted, however with no sign of understanding or an emotional connection. Observant of each other's actions and progress without a definite intention to unite, hardly could we decide to be more than just the school pals. We were only a part of the large group, the ends of the chord.

Apart, but we could sense the emotions brewing inside our minds that became the foundation of the US. How unusual it is to figure out the inner energy and decipher it!

A real connection is felt in-depth, in the profound meaning of a relationship lies the essence.

A little known,

a lot felt.

A lot more to know!

You covered half,

I walked the rest,

to make the two ends

ONE!

It was 2006 or 2007 when we officially united. We counted on each other. The second chance became a bliss. Yes, it was a second chance in the friendship that worked well. It turned out to be a soothing experience for us. Though being at different tangents some time we agreed with each other, the beginning was quite tough, we were filling spaces and wondered if we could be each other's comfort company. But we proved to be a good company, a wise friendship that made us better every day as an individual, as a student, and as friends.

Since then, it has a part and parcel of every emotion in life. Too many years, till eternity, the classical tale will be alive with a new story in every phase, uniqueness in its exhibition yet a single emotion.

Round The Earth!

Every minute, second or a mini second that counts on this earth are a token to the time spent in togetherness. Round the Earth, you are a beautiful flower, that I water daily.

CHAPTER 5: WE GOT IT

We got that the concern, care, emotional connect and love was real, the support system was present to sustain our lives, we got each other. No relationship ever comes easy, nor it is hard to get into the skin of it. It is an enduring journey of patience, perseverance, hardships and core love. It was a simple, evolving relationship with a nature of its own, the beauty of the world and experience, an ounce to make it prominent and notably distinct of its time.

We were a moment close but the other in an odd to settle our belief and build trust, a year-long trial that made our friendship sustainable and forever fresh. A recap of the year it all started, 2007!

So we started as classmates, among a heterogeneous group and initiated a step towards each other, beginning with a sweet and formal take on this ride. We never knew where the acquaintance would lead us to, we never had any perceptions nor expectations of how a perfect relationship should be. The simplicity of the time dwelled in us subtly and in a fine process, that refined our friendship at each stage.

There were disagreements and small fights, but we ended up talking somehow, no matter prolonged, friendship always got our back. Our daily routine got the most essential details of our friendship, life and beyond. Among the group of many, we had a chord connecting us. We began to accompany each other, sharing thoughts and memories, shared our progress and failure. Among the host of situations that life could put us in, it did and we stood with each other like rock, firmly balancing our obstacles.

How it felt walking together, I don't remember, our footsteps know our distance, but our mind only remembers the memories it has borne.

It was not enough,

my childhood was just not enough

to be a happy go lucky person.

The days were easily countable,

had I not known the numbers,

I would not have counted my

days remaining of my

Childhood!

Had it been just enough of the time with you,

I would not have time and again

gone to the years by,

to roll back what we,

Stepped out of.

It could not be enough,

My childhood was not enough.

But,

It was sufficiently large

to be with you.

CHAPTER 6: LET'S TAKE A WALK

The bonfire was lit,

the woods gave room warmth and light

It was cold as the Arctic,

It was a merry season,

and the new year was round the corner.

The town was prepping festive feast.

Excitement and happiness was common on

the face.

And my flavourful pleasure,

a marshmallow with her.

All I could ask for one moment, please.

Fondly I remember,

A day,

a fine day at school,

I circled a new word in my dictionary,

RESOLUTION

I too had to make one.

Silently, in two different minds,

they made their promises,

As I seek to travel in the past,

I drive my way to the paths and lanes

where we once shared our words

And the finest promises of the time!

Before 2008 bid us goodbye, we were each other's confidants and well-wishers. We were growing, our aspirations and goals were getting wider, so were a few fantasies rolling on our minds. Everything was aligned. But life had its script and we were the role players, plotted in different situations. The concluding bells of 2008 were cherishing and rejoicing and we were immersed in our celebration of being the most healthy competitors and companions, it was a fun pouring moment.

We were the protagonist of our stories in our respective situations, we had to face the reality of a thin line (wall) separation, we no longer had the comfort of class partners, the right was snapped. The break time used to be a soothing time, 20minutes to compensate for a long lonely day.

The solitude of two years, however could not part ways. Standing firm on the testimony of friendship, the trial of distance, the separation that career gave us, a bit of difference in thoughts, disagreements, confusions, petty fights, and few childish acts, we made it.

Defying the odds, we stood together, getting better each passing day like an old wine.

Here I raise,

A toast,

to the vintage time,

to the warm memories,

that is my old school companions.....

the gift of life

and humbleness of the sky.

HARSHIT SRIVASTAVA

Harshit Srivastava, an engineer by profession and a poet by heart. He got his debut poetry book published in Feb 2020 titled "Maryadit Ram". His poetries have deep faith in the learning and ethics of Ramayana. His wish to pen down all his knowledge acquired from the Holy Hindu Scriptures has brought him to this level

available at

amazon

Google
Books

अहिल्या उद्धार

भूमिका:— अहिल्या उद्धार के प्रसंग को कवि द्वारा मानवीय दृष्टिकोण से लिखने का प्रयास किया गया है।

दिखी एक उजड़ी सी बगिया।
वीरान पड़ी शापित सी कुटिया।।
बिन पानी के दिखे तलइया ।
पोत चलें न बिना खिवइया ।।
बिन आत्मा के जीव थे सारे।
बादल से नहीं दिखते तारे ।।
चन्दा बिना आकाश हो कैसे।
बिन सीरत सूरत हो जैसे ।।
सूरज बिना जीवन है कैसे।
मछली सब बिन नीर के जैसे।।

एक बेबस सी दिखी थी नारी।
कभी बहुत थी पति को प्यारी।।
ऋषि गौतम की पत्नी अहिल्या।
पति चरणों में देखत दुनिया।।
इन्द्र प्राप्त पद कामुक राजा।
चाहा करन कुकर्म अभागा।।
पड़ी दृष्टि अहिल्या पर कैसे।
चतुर शेर देखे मृग जैसे।।
पापी ने मुनि वेष बनाया।
अकेले पड़ी अहिल्या को पाया।।
किया कुकर्म इन्द्र ने ऐसे।
चोर धनी को ठगे हो जैसे।।
ऋषि गौतम इतने में आये।
पत्नी को उस दशा में पाये।।
सब कुछ भाँप गये मुनिराजा।
बना नपुंसक इन्द्र अभागा।।
कामी पुरूष का हाल हो कैसे।
जले कीट दीपक में जैसे।।

अहिल्या को अब समझ में आया।

पापी ने क्या जाल बिछाया।।

देर बहुत हो चुकी थी तब तक।

त्रेता युग में लुटी एक अस्मत।।

वह रोई और बहुत गिड़गिड़ाई।

बिना गलती के सजा थी पाई।।

मुनि क्रोध में कुछ नहीं देखा।

बुद्धि, विवेक अग्नि में फेंका ।।

क्रोध ज्ञान को कैसे खाये ।

अग्नि जैसे सब वस्त्र जलाये।।

दारा त्याग मुनि बोले ऐसा ।
            अरे कलंकिनी से संबंध हो कैसा।।
इन्द्र संसर्ग से पापिन है तू ।
            हर प्रकार से त्यागिन है तू ।।
हाँ तुझे एक पापिन मानता हूँ।
            अभी इसी क्षण तुझे त्यागता हूँ ।।
पति बिना नारी तन कैसे   ।
            पानी बिना नदियाँ हो जैसे ।।
सोम बिना सुन्दर तन ऐसे ।
            सुहाग बिना दुल्हन हो जैसे।।

नाथ क्षमा, कह वह गिड़गिड़ाई।
पति को हर तरह से समझाई।।
मगर मुनि आवेश में आकर ।
कर दिया पूरा आश्रम श्राप वश।।
नाथ नहीं मैं तनिक भी दोषी।
यह घटना मात्र समय की पोषी।।
वक्त रचित घटना, कौन समझ पाएगा।
ऐसी स्त्री,बता कौन अपनाएगा।।
किन्तु मैं तुझे वचन हूँ यह देता।
कोई धर्मात्मा है यह कहता।।
तू नहीं है दोषी,नहीं कलंकनी ।
मैं सहर्ष तुझे बनाऊँगा संगनी।।

ऋषि विश्वामित्र बोले कुछ ऐसा।
पृथ्वी पर नहीं कोई राम के जैसा।।
राम अवध की हो तुम आत्मा ।
तुमसे बड़ा नहीं कोई धर्मात्मा ।।
आग्रहपूर्वक मेरी बात सुनो तुम।
ऋषि पत्नी से बात करो तुम ।।

राम बहुत सोचे औ मुस्काये।
मुनि स्त्री के चरणों में धाये।।
अवगुन एक इन्द्र दर्शाया ।
काम प्रगट परस्त्री पर आया।।
गौतम ऋषि मुनि विज्ञानी ।
इन्द्र को सजा देने की ठानी।।
माँ इसमें कुछ गलत न देखूँ।
मैं भी इन्द्र पर ही लानत भेजूँ।।
पर माँ तुमने सीमा न लाँघी।
फिर किस बात बनी अपराधी।।
हाँ, मैं रघुकुल दशरथ का बेटा।
ऋषि गौतम से बहुत हूँ छोटा।।

किन्तु जो सत्य मैं वही कहूँगा।
तुम्हें त्यागने वाले ऋषि की नहीं सुनूँगा।।
यह समाज की रीति अनोखी।
पुरूष की गलती पर स्त्री दोषी।।
पुरूष समाज का प्रतिनिधित्व करता हूँ।
सबकी तरफ से क्षमा माँगता हूँ।।
ऋषि गौतम के पास चलो तुम।
माँ उनको अब क्षमा करो तुम।।
नारी है सब समाज का गहना।
इससे बड़ी न दूसर रचना।।
ऋषि हैं दोषी तुम्हें क्षमा करेंगें।
अपने हृदय में फिर रख लेगें।।

गौतम नारि श्राप बस उपल देह धरि धीर,
चरण कमल रज चाहति कृपा करहु रघुबीर।

सुनत कोमल श्रीराम की वाणी।
			आँखों में आ गया पानी।।
वो पानी अपमान में आया ।
			यह पानी सम्मान से आया।।

दूर कहीं मेघों को देखकर जैसे धरती मुस्काती है,
पारस के स्पर्श मात्र से मिट्टी सोना बन जाती है,
वैसे ही विश्वास प्रेम से हर स्त्री सम्मानित हो जाती है।।

राम नाम के दो अक्षर ने कितनों का बेड़ा पार किया।
हाँ कौशल्या के जाये बेटे तुमने मेरा उद्धार किया।।
राम तुम्हारी सोच अगर यह दुनिया अपनाएगी।
फिर कोई अभागिन अहिल्या कभी न त्यागी जाएगी।।

विश्वामित्र बीच में बोले ।
      ऋषि गौतम की बात वो खोले।।
बहन अहिल्या सुनो अब मुझसे।
      गौतम ऋषि नहीं दूर हैं तुमसे।।
यहीं पास है हिमालय पर्वत।
      वहीं मुनि रहते तपस्यारत।।
अभी मैं अपना शिष्य बुलाऊँगा।
      तुम्हें मुनि के पास पहुँचाऊँगा।।
वह जाकर मुनि को सब बतलाएगा।
      श्रीराम के विचार उन्हें सुनाएगा।।
वचनबद्ध मुनि तुम्हें निहारकर।
      गलती अपनी सुधारेगें तुम्हें अपनाकर।।

विश्वामित्र राम को देखे।
गये समीप बोले कुछ ऐसे।।
निर्गुण रूप से भल हैं रामा।
समदर्शी सब पूरनकामा।।
पतितों का उद्धार करें जो।
पूजन के भी योग्य बने वो।।

।। जय श्रीराम।।

MISS KAMLANI

Writing is my passion. I love to write poems, stories. I love to read a lot. Everything that includes creativity attracts me the most.

I have my stories published in two Anthologies:

- Salad days, A saunter by Poetry World.org

- Colour of Dreams by Yoalfaaz.

I also write on my ideas on my blog :

misskamlani.blogspot.com

I always participate in writing competitions. My story was also published in Vadilal's story contest in its October 2017 calendar.

This is why I decided to become a freelancer content writer.

From 2012 till 2017, I used to write blogs for IT companies.

But, I didn't see the growth that I wanted. Hence, I decided

to switch to another topic for writing. So, now I am

accepting projects from every industry except IT.

Apart from writing, I deeply care for the environment, my

Mother Earth.

For this reason, I volunteered with World Around You, an

eco-friendly product manufacturer firm in Free theTrees

campaign where we used to remove the nails from the

trees.

I am also associated with Ecofemme as an ambassador for

the Menstrual Organic Cloth pad programme.

I love to do activities that can teach me something new,

something unique. I always strive to learn. Travel and

adventure is yet another thing that I am mad at.

SEVEN WONDERS OF THE WORLD

To know what exactly creativity is, a glimpse of
these creations is enough,

To know at what heights human beings can reach; a
small snap of these creations is enough,

To know that difficult things are always possible;
inspiration from these wonders is enough.

To know what motivation is, the story of their
creators is enough.

To know how deep the feelings can be, a visit to that
place is a must.

MEN AND WOMEN

When men are in tension women pays attention,

She gives him some prevention,

That helps him to reduce stress extension,

And enjoy life with full attention,

Along with his lady love; who renders every solution.

SWEET SEASON RAINY SEASON

Best season for lovers, for poets

Mostly liked by all

The cool climate brings freshness and peace to

mind

Breathe and life for our Mother Earth.

Brings new creative thoughts in the poet's mind

Dark clouds thunder like a lion's roar

Lightning appears as,

It seems nature taking photographs

Of beautiful Earth wearing green saree

God's great boon,

Makes atmosphere pleasant

Provides happiness

Gives coolness to the eyes

Increases romance between love birds

Can be called as Romantic Season

The unique season where nature's

Great "rainbow" is seen

Seven colored vibgyor

Asks us to live

A colorful and joyful life.

SMILE

When you want to make someone happy,

Just give a SMILE.

When you want to become beloved of all;

Just give a SMILE.

Even a very sad person or lonely person

becomes happy,

With a little smile of yours.

Give a little smile whenever someone

looks at you.

Don't show bad expressions,

As this reveals your nature.

A little small and sweet smile makes

everyone happy.

People think you are a Happy Fellow,

And you are always happy in your Life.

Don't show Anger but Give a Smile.

It gives Peace to someone's heart.

Always keep smiling in your Life,

And be Happy.

Be a healer, not a killer.

O' SWEET NIGHT

The night is full of darkness and peace

As night is our friend;

Twinkling stars and

Shining moon

Are friends of night.

The night of spring season

Is a special type;

The cool breeze and soft wind

Blow during the night.

They give us happiness and peace.

The night is very peaceful.

So, I wish to remain awake

At night and enjoy its peace

Sweet birds and animal sleep

Quietly in their nests;

The nature is very quiet and

Calm at night

I like this quietness of our

Nature at night

That's why I love this poem

Named "O Sweet Night".

SUICIDE

When an irrespective thing occurs in

Person's life;

He gets depressed becomes sad or moody

He feels himself to be guilty and feels

shameful;

During these situations a person thinks to

do suicide, to free from tensions.

Such cases lead a person to commit

suicide.

When one becomes helpless finds no way

to come out of the difficulty;

One commits suicide just to free oneself

from difficulties.

A student commits suicide when he thinks

that he will not be able to show good

performance in its school,

So, to free from scolding it commits

suicide.

When one is facing odd days in life, faces

poverty;

When one is in depression due to

loneliness or the great loss in business then he

commits suicide.

But suicide is not the right way to come

out from difficulties;

One who commits suicide is not able to

face the mountain like

Problems' occurring in one's life

Is considered a coward person.

Suicide means to make our soul roam

here and there up to the next 7 births.

So, dear friends please face problems

bravely and don't commit suicide.

It is a great loss to our soul and also to our

next birth.

THE RAINY SEASON

The Rainy season is full of dark and white clouds.

Rainy season brings peace and happiness.

All the people are satisfied with the rain.

The rain is like a breathe,

People breathe air to live.

In the same way,

The earth breathes the rain to live.

Rain brings good thoughts to the poet's mind.

Rainy season makes the atmosphere peaceful.

Rainy season makes the plants greener

And the gardens look beautiful.

The Rainy season is like a boon to the earth.

That satisfies the thirsty farmers

As well as all living beings on the Mother Earth.

THE RELATIONS

The Relation, a bond that binds;

Two persons with affection or love,

Relations i.e. precious jewels

Created by nature,

Smooth by birth;

But becomes rough when kept in

Contact with anger, pride, greed, etc.

The Relation between mother and child is;

A true bond of love and sacrifice,

A true bond of trust and belief between

Husband and wife,

A true bond of trust and knowledge between

Guru and its disciple.

A true bond of affection between

Brothers and sisters.

Real attachment of justice and truth between

God and His devotee.

The Perfect combination of hardships

between

Joys and sorrows.

A true bond of peace between

Nature and morning i.e. dawn

A true bond of silence between

Nature and night

Relations are soft as flowers,

Destroys when caused a little harm.

Must be followed with great care;

To avoid any disturbances.

Which may lead them to an end.

SEX

Sex is a word to differentiate males and females.

It is not a bad word or a very cheap word,

mostly understood by today's generations.

It is made cheap due to blue films, cheap

posters, some scenes in films and websites, etc.

Things shown in blue films are sex

relationships but not sex.

Sex is known as "Jaati" in Gujarati and we

call it "ling" in Hindi.

There is a bad impact on children's mind

due to these blue films,

Certain websites negatively demonstrate Sex

This brings the assumption "Sex means

intimacy" which is wrong.

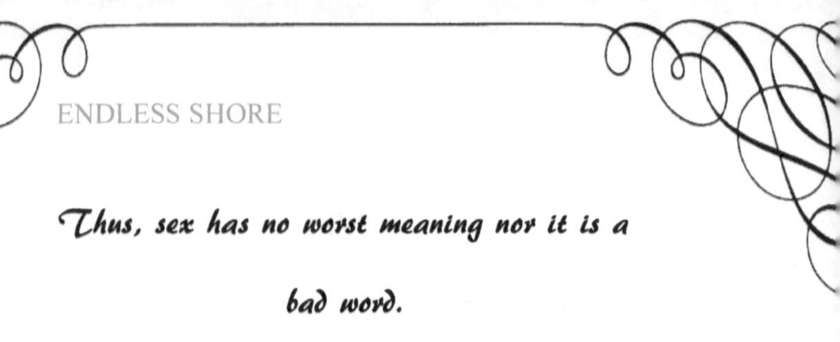

Thus, sex has no worst meaning nor it is a

bad word.

Sex is not sexy but simple.

So, whenever you hear this word don't

get ashamed

But make people aware of its true

meaning.

BIRDS

Sing Birds,

Sing Sweet Songs,

And make the morning

Cool and pleasant-

Oh! Sweet birds,

Awake the world early with your sweet voice;

As the sun is going to set,

In the evening;

And the night is nearing;

Soon the sun will get,

In the west.

And it will become a dark night.

Oh! Sweet birds,

Go to your nests quickly,

As you will be the ones,

Obeying the nature's rules

And awake this world

On the early cool morning.

WHAT IS LIFE?

How flowers are made we don't know!

How we are made we don't know!

How this world is made that also we don't

know!

But one thing we know, that we are living a type

of thing in this world.

What is that thing do you know?

That thing is 'life' itself.

What is the life we don't know?

Some live life in a simple way.

While some live life in a fantastic way.

OR, some live life in a very sad way.

I am saying that "Life is a type of puzzle".

Solving this puzzle is a very difficult task.

Some while solving it is solving very easily.

While some are failing to solve this puzzle.

Those who are trying to solve this puzzle

through hard work,

They are getting success in their work;

otherwise, they are failing to do their

work.

At last, I would say that "Try to solve this

hardest puzzle".

You will be in the highest position in your life.

JOHANNES KRAISLER

Johannes Kraisler, a poet who uses this pen name is a musician in soul and artist in life, gets inspiration from life. A person who loves to read books, especially classics, historical and fantasy. Loves to be in harmony with nature.

Published works:

Co-author in "Shades Of Pain In Her Eyes".

Guest Editor of "Dreams Defined" anthology.

CHOICE

I had my finger on the trigger... Was going to shoot.

He has killed my daughter... Has killed ten young girls more.

I knew him... His name has been published in the newspapers and not one time only... His sad story of life...

He defiled eleven girls, defiled and cruelly killed... Killed my Sarah too...

Her image I saw in his eyes, for a moment fierce hatred arose in my heart... and I shot...

Fired on...

First time in life I killed a HUMAN...

But I got revenge for my daughter... Revenged an injustice... Stopped the murderer...

Stopped the murderer but became the murderer myself...

I left the judge place with the unseeing eyes... His blood left the trace on my shoes... on my hands... in my heart...

I knew that i have done right. I have stopped him. Henceforth no one will suffer anymore from his hand. And I got a revenge for my daughter's honour...

I walked down the street still with the gun in my hand... Was going and didn't see where to go...

I did right, I saved lives of many other innocent victims, he could defile. But I didn't feel peace in my soul...

His death didn't calm my heart down... didn't return my daughter to me...

I felt that I'm falling somewhere in a dark chasm... Meanwhile there was the dawn outdoor... The sun let his first shiny rays walk everywhere... Suddenly I've heart the birds' singing... Noticed all green leaves on the trees... Life is so beautiful, so filled... Everywhere was peace...

But there was no peace in my soul... There was the darkness only... Darkness and nothing else...

Everything around reminded about divine essence... Everywhere was the divine imprint... Same divine spark there is in people too... In each person... In him also it was... He got his life not without the reason... He also had some mission... But I took his gift...

Did I have any right to take life if it was not me who gave it?.. He killed my daughter... I got the revenge... But this didn't return her back to me...

With her death a lot of sorrows came in our family... My wife still is crying during nights... And I had sworn that I would find him and will revenge...

Police didn't know anything... couldn't find any trace. I also was searching for a long time... But finally I found. Came to know about the address . He was living alone. His wife left him after death of their child - girl... Suppose, she was a victim of an act of brigandage... As I read in a newspaper, in Court he told: "Is it justly, that she died... Girls of her age are enjoying life... And she is dead...". Justly... And is it justly to take other's lives?.. But I also took...

I thought that his death would bring me relief... But it didn't...

Did she wish him to die?.. Did she wish me to sully my hands and her bright memory with a lot of blood?.. He was a miscreant... but still he was a human... He also suffered...

She died, but maybe her soul is still alive?..

NO! NOT LIKE THIS!!!

Her body died but soul is eternal... He couldn't hurt her soul.. It means that she didn't die...

This recognition has brought light to my heart... But didn't dispel the darkness there...

Revenge is not a justification of murder... Revenge is a daughter of angerness, and angerness doesn't bring peace to the soul...

Death of one person won't resurrect the other one...

***

I had my finger on the trigger... Was going to shoot.

But this would not bring the relief...

And I took my finger off that trigger...

***

I called the police and gave them all important information. The Court sentenced him for life imprisonment...

We don't have right to take someone's life, as there were not us who gave it...

NITIN CHOPRA

Dr. Nitin Chopra, from Panipat, India is a passionate poet and an aspiring doctor. Let alone in the arms of nature, stream of words cascade through his verses, that robs the hearts of many. He believes a gentle and caring heart reaches great heights. He is a crazy traveller learning from the life's experiences. Because of his habit & the hunger to learn new stuff he is a Google certified Digital and Content Marketer.

He's a down to earth person with tremendous achievements. He has been published in various International journals, E-books and Magazines. He was ranked one under top read poets list (under 20 year age group) with 3,50,000 plus votes worldwide, all thanks to lovely readers. He has also received appreciation letters from the Late Dr.A.P.J. Abdul Kalam (Former President Of India) and actor Raj Babbar for his literary works.

He can be contacted at

http://facebook.com/nitinpoet

http://Instagram.com/nitinchoprapoet

देश में गुज़री शामें

आँखों में अश्क़ों के अम्बार छोड़ जाती हैं

देश में गुज़री शामें यारों मुझको बहुत सताती हैं।

रूठे हैं हम उनसे, पर वो कहाँ रूठे हैं

यही तो समझाने वो हर शाम चली आती हैं।

वो मीठी मीठी भूख में, माँ के हाथों की रोटी

आज भी भूखा सोता हूँ, तो मुझको जगाने आती हैं।

देर से घर आने पर, पापा की वो डाँट

आज भी देर लगाऊँ तो, मुझको समझाने आती हैं

देश की अल्हड़ गलियों से, यारों की प्यारी आवाज़ें

आज भी तन्हा होता हूँ, तो मुझको बुलाने आती हैं।

वो बरसते सावन, वो भीगी माटी की ख़ुशबू

आज भी मस्त हवाओं में, साज़ कई घुल जाते हैं।

वो घर, वो आँगन, वो गुज़री हुई बातें यारों

आज भी परदेस में मुझको रुलाने आती हैं।

आँखों में अश्क़ों के अम्बार छोड़ जाती हैं

देश में गुज़री शामें यारों मुझको बहुत सताती हैं।

रूठे हैं हम उनसे, पर वो कहाँ रूठे हैं

यही तो समझाने वो हर शाम चली आती हैं।

LIFE OF BUTTERFLY

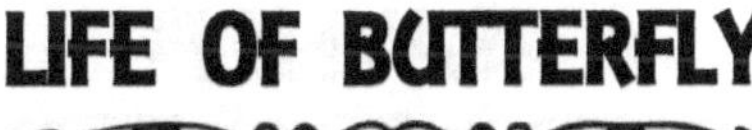

It's hard for me,

to break this shell covering me

They say it's important for me to break it myself,

Otherwise I wont evolve, it's my future key

But it's breaking me, it's taking me

It's making me dry, making me die.

They say that once I come out,

I'll have beautiful wings.

But, dear gardener,

What if I end up in these strings?

A TRAVELLER

(Continuation of "life of a butterfly")

Sitting in shades of that army's stolen shed

I think about that crazy butterfly

Fluttering hard to get her wings

Making her life tough

People made her rough

Teaching her, how to fly,

Did we forget, she can die?

Dear gardener, you told us

Once she comes out she will have beautiful wings,

And, I told you,

What if she dies in these strings?

Imagine, think, decide... she still swings

Thinking of you, to save her

Help her, support her

We know you (today's world) are crazy!!

But believe her,

Please don't deceive her!

DR.NIVEDITHA

Dr. Niveditha MDS., a dentist by profession and a writer by passion. Little scribble on the pages and inked verses as the time ages, has brought her to this position of her life.

From being no one to a person with such important position, all praises goes to the Lord and Poetry World Org.

Without Dr. Rohit, Nitin Chopra and the whole team she would not be where she is.

Gratitude to my family and PWO.

She writes under the pen name Kyra and is currently working on her solo book. She has been published as a co-author in various anthologies and was also the editor of 'Salad Days – A Saunter' and 'Jeremiad Of Hearts' published by PWO.

Follow her writings

Instagram : nivy_dr

UPCOMING BOOK

available at

SERENDIPITY

Darkest dreams,

Deepest scars,

Painful screams,

Never ending terrors.

Agonising memories,

In my abyss called life,

The way I found you,

Is serendipity.

Be it luck,

Or destiny,

The way I found you,

Is pure serendipity.

A hand to hold on,

I shall always provide,

A shoulder to lean on,

You shall always find.

Moments with you,

Made my life anew,

Merry smiles and laughter,

Without you would be few.

Oh, my dear,

Come, let's explore together,

Let not this journey end,

For, I shall be your comforter.

With no expectations let's lead,

This life to a better place,

With no thoughts of future,

To the end let's race.

Oh, my dear! In you, I shall always be.

REMEMBER ME?

Hand in hand they sat,

Losing themselves in each other's gaze.

Wrinkled skin and greying hair,

Expressed their withering age.

A warm and comfy hand she placed,

Assuring her love till her heart ceased.

Tears brimmed her depressed eyes,

As memories of moments together, flashed.

"Do you remember me?" - she asked,

To her amnesiac husband, who sat aghast.

Unspoken words, answered her query,

While the eyes that shone,

Revealed his concealed love story.

DESTINED DESIRES

She found it hard, to let him go,
Though it was hard, he let her go.

Letting it go was the worst,
As rivers of tears had burst.

It'd crushed them to the core,
Making their hearts roar.

They desired for more,
But, destiny wouldn't favour.

Elixir of his life, she was,
The blood of her heart, he was.

Together they made a great pair,
But life had always been unfair.

In their eyes, the world could perceive,

Their love that was concealed.

Neither of them had asked,

What their hearts had masked.

Fearing of losing each other,

They stayed as friends together.

The days neared its end,

Marking a scar that'd never blend.

With sad smiles they did depart,

As they were fated to be apart.

Many years had passed,

Yet, their hearts never surpassed.

OM MANGLA

Om Mangla who lives in twincity Yamunanagar is a 17 year old writer doing his +2 from DpS, Yamunanagar. His passion is writing down his thoughts. He loves reading and watching movies.. he has been published as a co-author in many anthologies

DARTA KYU HAI TU BHOOT SE

Darta kyu hai tu pret se

Darna hai to dar us manav se

Jo darta nahi balatkar karne se

Jo darta nahi Qanoon se

Nahi Darta kisi bhagwan se

Jo banata hai rangoli manav ki hi lashon se

Jo khelta hai holi tujh jaise ke lahu sai

Dar mat bhoot sai nahi pret sai, Darna hai to dar bas manav

kai is roop sai

EK BAAR HAAR KAR HAR MAT JANA

Ek baar haar kar haar mat man jana

Haar sikha kar hi to jaati hai

Aapko sudharne ka moqa de jaati hai

Aapko jeet ki qeemat bata jati hai

Ruknaa mat pryaas karte rehna

Apne aap ko or behtar banana

Bas haar sai mat ghabrana

Ek baar haar kar har mat jana

QUOTES

नशा मत कर बंदिया तू लूट जाएगा ,

कुछ समय की ख़ुशी के ख़ातिर सारी उमर के लिए मर जाएगा

नशा करना ही है तो इश्क़ का कर जो तुझे सारी उमर उम्र नचाएगा

तू चाहकर भी होश माई ना आ पाएगा

ओ मेरे बरखुरदार थोड़ी कर ले अपने पर

भी मेहर

यहाँ करता नहीं कोई किसी की फिक्र

इस जाली दुनिया पर डाल एक नज़र

तेरे सफ़र में नहीं है कोई और हमसफ़र

ओह मेरे बरखुरदार थोड़ी कर लें अपनी भी फिक्र

अगर कुछ करने कि चाह रखते हो

आगे बढ़ने का दम रखते हो

तो दूरियाँ मत देखना

कठिनाइयाँ मत देखना

पैरों पर पड़े मेहनत के छालों के दर्द का मत सोचना

कोई क्या कहता है ये भी मत सोचना

कुछ देखना तो बस अपने सपनो को साकार होता देखना

कुछ सोचना तो बस यही सोचना की हमने नहीं है रुकना

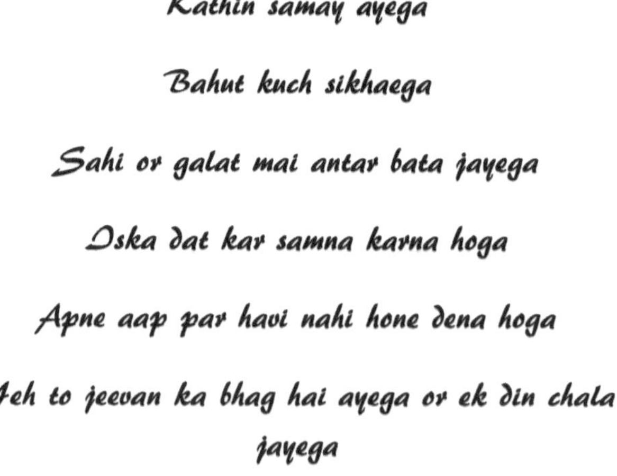

Kathin samay ayega

Bahut kuch sikhaega

Sahi or galat mai antar bata jayega

Iska dat kar samna karna hoga

Apne aap par havi nahi hone dena hoga

Yeh to jeevan ka bhag hai ayega or ek din chala jayega

Pata nahi ye zindagi kab kisse mila rahi hai

Achoon se mila kar achi yaadein bana rahi hai

Or Buroon se mila kar or mazboot bana rahi hai

Chahe kisi se bhi mila rahi hai par kuch to seekha
rahi hai ..

Tere Ishq mai dooba rehta tha

Teri chahat mai marta rehta tha

Par bahut bahut shukriya Apni auqat dikhane ke liye
Mujhe

hoosh mai laney kay liye

Sahi hi suna tha aaj dekh bhi liya

Mohabbat bhi dhoka de jati hai

Mohabbat karne wale ki auqat dikha jati hai

Bus ek dosti hi aise chez hai jo

Toot Kar bhi jud jati hai Auqat bhi nahi dikhati hai

Jab hum tumse baat karte thy

To bas baaton mai hi Khoo jaatey thy

Bhool Jaatey thy ke Tumhari Zindagi mai bahut
humse bhi

zaruri thy

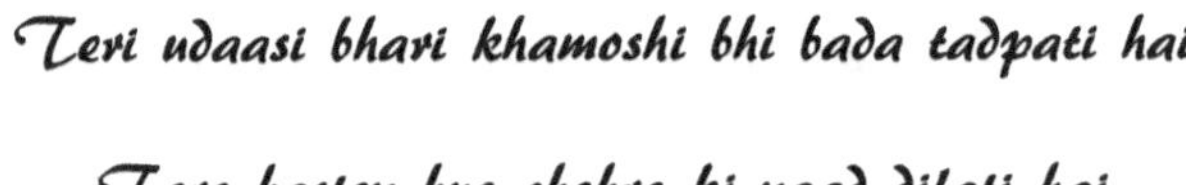

Teri udaasi bhari khamoshi bhi bada tadpati hai

Tere hastey hue chehre ki yaad dilati hai

PAKEEZA RIZVI

Pakeeza Rizvi, born on 27th august 1992 is a vehement poet from Karachi, Pakistan. She has done her masters in philosophy from the University of Karachi. She is a versatile poet who loves to write in Persian, English and Urdu. Sufism which means divine love has touched her so much, that most of her poems are based on that same. One could see the philosophy of drop and sea in her sufi poems.

Poetry is not her interest but her breath. Poetry means a lot for her like her life. She believes, her verses that would remain forever in the hearts of the readers would be her greatest achievement in her life. She has been a part of the anthologies "Open Your Eyes" and "Shades Of Pain In Her Eyes"

Follow her writings at

https://www.facebook.com/Shayari-By-Pakeeza-Rizvi-1813258658901086/?ref=bookmarks

PASSENGER OF LOVE

In a silent valley of feelings,

Under the shadow of deep emotions,

A person with a bag of old memories,

With a bundle of unsolved queries,

Waiting for his next journey,

Beyond this inner world,

He is a passenger of love,

In the crowd of heartless people,

He has lost everything,

But his broken dreams and hopes,

Still with him as a mate,

No one understands his unspoken words,

He is a passenger of love,

The hope of new dawn in his eyes,

He does not sleep all the night,

Besides his innocent smile,

A lot of griefs alive,

How much alone he is,

Sing a sad song like a dove,

He is a passenger of love,

His eyes searching for his destiny,

Long wait reduces his ambitions,

But his courage is as strong as mountains,

Cool breeze never effected him,

Died before dead,

No one scattered him,

He knows how to tuck,

He is a passenger of love.

SACRED BIRD

Seeds and Grains are the food of other one's,

O'comrade you are the sacred bird,

Your food and sup are nothing but love

So, eat love and drink love,

That is the best sustenance for your body

And the best nutrients for your heart.

O'BELOVED WHERE WILL YOU MEET

Happiness or grief

No matter what the seasons bring

In autumn,

In spring,

Only for you he sings

That song like a lamentation

unceasingly flowing from his lips,

"Far from the meadows or far from the streets

O'Beloved where will you meet

In search of you

A shepherd lost in the flock of sheep"

AN INNOCENT PRISONER'S LIFE

An innocent prisoner in the cage,
Waits to pass his age,
he Writes something on a page,
i think those are count of the days,
Which he's spending in the cage,

when the sun begins to set,
He sits on the piece of land,
Holds something in his hand,
Which is cracked and wrecked,
I think those are his family snaps,

His eyes are full of tears,
His heart is full of fears,
His only companions today,
Else No one sees him and hears,
He has been alone about many years,

He is like that silent picture,
With whom he shares his grief,
To get some peace to get some relief,
All around is darkness of cruelty,
Every one see him as guilty,

No one know that he is innocent,
He has no lawyer and no cents,
He did n't commit any crime,
But his calmness and poorness wasted all his time,

His moans and groans won't live forever,
His tears and fears will disappear,
No one will tease him, no one will beat him,
When he leaves this world,
And one day God will show the truth to this world,
He will break the silence and prove his sinlessness,

This is the truth and this is the fact,
His silence will shout again and again,
He was innocent, innocent by any law and act,
So why did his life go dreaded in the cage.

IN YOUR LOVE

O' Beloved In your love

My odorless wilted heart

Became amaranth rose

you adorned and saturated it with care

Now it blooms with your name

and it's your fragrance that comes from it.

PRITI KANWAR SHEKHAWAT

Priti Kanwar born in Chirawa, Rajashthan, 24 years old working in a banking sector has a knack of writing poems and love quotes since the last 3 years. She has a MBA from Amity University, and has been living in Delhi since the last 4 years and has been actively writing and posting about her own feelings and events that have changed her outlook towards life.

She writes poems which many can relate to because most of the people can't pen down their thoughts which rapidly go on in their minds.

She is a well versed poet and her work is adored and admired by many.

She has just finished writing her solo book which features about 24 poems. She is a God fearing person and loves to enjoy even the smallest things life has to offer, she has a bubbly nature & strong personality and wants to make her parents proud by writing poems and quotes that may inspire many in the future.

You can follow her at priti0604 Insta ID

YOU ARE SUNSHINE

You are sunshine

On this selfless world

just wipe your tears and don't cry

Here nobody heard

So, now tie your waist and let's fly so high

Only you can decide why are you alive

just put a smile and take a good vibe

Nobody cares, why are you crying?

so, baby open your wings and take the risk

This time is yours

Don't be afraid of the heights,

just trust yourself and be ready to take a ride

Don't care for humans

Because God is on your side

yes, baby believe me!

only you are sunshine...

A GIRL IN THE DARK

She has a beautiful face without a name

With a cute smile, she can hide her pain

This girl in the dark.

The fake society you can't judge, what she wears

How she laughs, she doesn't want your fakeness

She gives you everything that you give her

She only wants a lovable and sweet hug

This girl in the dark.

The world,

Because of your fakeness

She is slowly dying

And now this girl again sits alone

She wants a place truly called home

This girl in the dark.

She wants nothing more than to be free

Don't judge her, how she looks

See what she is doing for us

She only needs love

That is what she deserves

This girl in the dark........

I WANT TO RESIGN

Sometimes I want to resign

So, I can listen to myself

What I am, what I was, what I will be

So I can understand my world

What I have to remember

What I have to forget

So, I can describe myself

What I want from my life

What I don't

So I can truly love myself and then someone else

I want to resign

From myself to join me.

IS THERE ANYTHING

Is there anything I want to share

sometimes I can't explain

Is there someplace I want to go

somewhere I can feel the rain

Is there something I have to clear

something which is this world can't

Is there some love and care I have

so I can give someone who needs it

Is there something I want to feel

some pain of yours which you can't explain

Is there some stories I want to tell

some dreams that may come true.

WHEN I AM IN THE RAIN

Feel so complete when I'm in the rain,

I feel no sorrow I feel no pain,

I may give me a cold but I don't care,

There's a calming sensation from grass to air,

The feeling of love I don't have, I will gain,

Because my heart falls open as I stand in the rain.

Here is something like a love trend,

It's about me it's about you,

It's about our life, like a storm before rain,

I feel so complete when I am in the rain...

MY SILENCE

My silence means I am tired of fighting

Now, there is nothing left to fight for,

My silence means I am tired of explaining myself,

and now I don't have any feelings left

My silence means I have adapted the changes in my
life,

and there is nothing to complain,

My silence means, now I am on my healing process,

I want to forget everything which I wanted from
anyone

My silence means, now I am ready to give my best
version.

NO REASON AT ALL

There is no reason to hold something

There is nothing to lose not even one thing,

we are beginning a world but for why

we don't know anything.

You can be rich with money

I can be poor with emotions,

In the end, both doesn't matter

I kept everything inside

what it meant to me

you opened up about

what's not belong to me,

we both are playing, but why

we don't know anything.

I want to go so far

There is nothing like war,

but we made a world

like a big and ugly scar,

I want to dwell in an ocean

with full of emotions,

still, we are fighting, we don't want to say it,

we knew it all, we want to ignore

it's just a bad, cold goodbye

Because it's true we don't know anything.

CLOUDY LIFE

Sometimes I think life is a digger,

and I'm like hell Earth,

Trying to keep me away,

to find a better way.

Isn't it so cloudy, rainy?

that makes us witty,

Maybe we have to fight more,

to get an invisible cure.

We are fighting from everyone and want to win,

finding a family and leaving our own,

we are living in a world where,

Every person wants to betray their guardians,

and nobody cares.

Do we want this?

Are we making this wish?

or just a diamond from outside, but full of ashes.

I KNEW YOU

I knew you,

I knew you from the touch of your rough hands,

I knew you to roast my innocent soul,

I knew you from every right to wrong since I was a child.

I knew you in every way you hurt me,

I knew you had nothing good for me,

I knew you were never ready

to know the reason why you did it.

I knew you wanted to hurt my skin,

but you broke my bones too,

I knew why you closed the doors I always wanted to open...

They said, stay away from the monsters

but they don't know one is living with them.....

K. RAMYA KALAIVANI

Hello! I am Ramya Kalaivani, hailing from the rich and beautiful city of Coimbatore, Tamil Nadu. I took up the pen at the age of 11 and as you can see, still can't set it down. I was drawn to Arts more than Tech and so here I am, pursuing my PhD in English. My love for my native language Tamil doesn't boil down and eventually made me prolific in Tamil write-ups too. As a result of my growing passion in News Reading, I am working as an RJ (Part Time) in All India Radio. Hey, you should tune in to me some day, it will be so much fun! I have also tried my hand on Carnatic Music.

If you give me more bragging rights - My literary profile made me as a Review Member in Journal of Emerging Technologies and Innovative Research; I've been the co-author of various anthologies. I am very fond of Nature and you will find most of my writings lean towards it. If there is one thing I believe stronger than anything, it is that nothing beats writing in conveying one's inner emotions to the world outside; and what other way to portray it than a magical poem?

I like to slide into my DMs, so ping me here-
Instagram ID: rjramyakalaivani

CEASELESS WARRIOR

Awakes first

To wake up the rest;

Single-cup of coffee

Acts as a toffee;

As if she has a hundred hands

She fulfills all demands;

All are gone for routine

She's lacking in her protein;

No one cares her intake

Even if she bakes the cake;

Never knew a slumber

Can make her bolster;

Joins laughter at fun

Gives shoulders when glum;

Sleeps after others

Still wakes up before others;

A mother is a great fighter

than a warrior

indeed!

SPURRED SHOOT

Farmer's toddler

Plant's psyche

Tutelage even in a wink of an eye.

After months of sweat and

Having transpired from the fierce world

Born these treasures,

Out of all pressures!

Comes out the fresh leaves

Even after the fallen ones!

Sometimes barren;

Sometimes blowy!

Still holding on with firm roots.

Visualize it in the wink of an eye;

Ponder it in the beat of heart!

IS ROSE A WEAPON?

He kneels

on the floor,

handing it

with glory.

Gazed she

beckons!

Isn't it

his weapon?

BABY'S SMILE

A piece of memory

she makes;

A piece of peace

she gives.

And I

Envision Heaven!

SNIPPETS

If you hadn't ignored me

I would've given you a healthy life!

- Agriculture

Funny interpretations and

Farcical innovations -

Facets of a fortuitous riddle!

Flower -

Encapsulates power of patience &

tactfulness of tenacity!

சிங்கப்பெண்ணே

பரந்து விரிந்த புவிக்கு
அவள் நாமம்!
கரைபுரண்டு ஓடும் நதிகளுக்கும்
அவள் பெயர்!
அன்பு, பாசம், கருணையின்
மொத்த உருவம் - அவள்!
அன்பான தேவதைகளை,
அலங்கோலப்படுத்தும் சிலர்!
மகிழ்ச்சியாய் சாலையில் அவள்
நிகழப்போவதை அறியாமல்!
அனைவரும் எமது சகோதரி என்று
உறுதிமொழி எடுப்பவன்
கற்பழிக்கிறான்!
குருதியை அவளிடம் கண்டவன்
திருப்தி அடைகிறான்
பின்விளைவுகளைப் பற்றி அறியாமல்!
அனாதையாய் அலங்கோலமாய்
சாலையோரத்தில் அவள் உடல்!
வாழ்க்கையின் இறுதிக் கட்டத்தில்,
பாசமான தாய் தந்தையர்
மனக்கண் முன் வர...
நிறைவேறாத ஆசைகள்
ஆசையாய் அழைக்க...
இறப்புக்கும் அவளுக்கும்
நடுவே போராட்டம்...
இறுதியில் யமதர்மன்

அவளை வென்று விட
அமைதியாய் உறங்கும் தன் உடலை
துடிதுடித்துப் பார்க்கிறது
அவள் ஆன்மா...
இதில் அஞ்சி நடுங்கி
முடங்கிப்போனவர்கள் பலர்!
இழந்துவிட்டோம் பல
கவிஞர்களையும், ஆசிரியர்களையும்
தலைவிகளையும்!
நாம் முடங்கிக் கிடந்த காலம்
மலையேறிவிட்டது!
தாமதம் செய்யாதே
விரைந்தெழு!
உறங்கிக் கிடந்தால்
விடியல் உன் வசமல்ல!
முடங்கிக் கிடந்தால்
பட்டுப்புழு
பட்டாம்பூச்சி ஆவதில்லை!
பாரதி கண்ட புதுமைப் பெண்ணாய் இருக்கட்டும் உன்
பயணம்!
வாழ்ந்து காட்டு!
அன்பு செலுத்துவதில்
அன்னை தெரசாவாக!
சாதனை புரிவதில்
கல்பனா சாவ்லாவாக!
விழித்தெழு பெண்ணே!,
புயலாய் மாறு!

மழைக்கு ஒரு மடல்

அகிலம் இரவாகிப்போக

அகத்தை அழகாக்கிடவே

வந்தாயோ வண்ண மழையே!

நனைந்த சாலைகளால்

நெகிழ்ந்தது நெஞ்சம்

சிந்திய துளிகளால்

சிறகடிக்குது மனம்!

கரையத் துடிக்கும் எந்தன் மனதினை

கட்டிப் போட்டே வைக்கிறேன்,

நீ முத்தமிடும் சத்தத்தால்

உறங்கிக் கொண்டிருக்கும் என் குழவி

விழித்திடும் என்பதால்!

சுடுமணலும் சில்லிடுமோ?

பிஞ்சு விரல் பாதங்கள்
சுடுமணலில் நடைபயில,
சாலையோரத்தில்
யாசகம்
கேட்டுக்கொண்டிருந்தாள்
அவன் 'தாய்'.

சிறுகுடல் பெருங்குடல்
போராட்டத்தில்
சுடுமணலும் அங்கே சில்லிட்டதோ?

இறுதிச்சடங்கு

இறந்து போன இதயத்திற்கு
இதழ்களை இறக்கவைத்து
மலர் வளையம்!

நிலா

கண் காணாத்தூரத்தில்
நீ இருந்தாலும்,
உன்னை
கைப்பிடிக்கவே ஏங்குது
மனம்!

கடல் அலை

நிலையற்ற வாழ்வை
நினைவுபடுத்தவே!
காலடித்தடங்களை
கரைசேர்க்க நீ விடுவதில்லையோ?

நிழல்

நித்தமும் உன்னுடன்
நிம்மதியாய் பயணிக்கிறேன்,
நிஜமில்லா என்னுடன்
நீங்காமல் இருக்கிறாய்,
நின் உருவத்துடன்
நிதர்சன உலகில் நானும்!

இப்படிக்கு,
நிழல்

SNEHA HEMBRAM

Sneha Hembram, born in Kolkata. Graduated in English Honours from Ravenshaw University, Cuttack, Odisha. Then pursued post graduation in Fashion Management Studies (FMS) from National Institute of Fashion Technology (NIFT), Kolkata.

She loves to write during her spare time, expressing her thoughts and emotions through words.

Instagram handle : whispers_of_soul_sh

Facebook : Sneha Hembram (Reena)

QUOTES

The Sun Shines With fire But Burning Itself

Similarly, To Give Others One Has to Bear the

Lose.

The new me was born,

When you destroyed

The whole of my...

Affection for you.

Sailing Away to Find the Treasure...

But What the Treasure Is?

And Where Is It?

Is It Somewhere In Other Land or

Buried Too Deep to Be Found

We Don't Know, Still Hoping to Find It

Life Is A Boat on Which We Sail

World Is the Huge Ocean

Hiding Treasure

When I see you next, you'll be the stranger with
whom I crossed the path unwillingly.

I don't recognize you as the person I ever use to
know you.

Because whom I used to know is dead and certainly
it's not

you for sure.

I'll wish never to meet you in any life cycle or era
the universe has.

VAMPIRE NEXT DOOR

We have recently shifted to the house of our forefathers. Due to some property dispute, my father came to resolve it.

Our house is located in a remote place far away from the city in the woods. It would be approximately 200kms from the main city.

A few distance away, there was one more house which was visible from my bedroom - 'The Haunted House'. It used to be my grandma's room. When I was a child I loved to sleep with my grandma.

From childhood, I was so curious about that house. Once I asked my grandma "Who's house is it? Why is it so quiet out there?"

In reply, Dida said, "That house is cursed. No one lives there. It devours every person who has ever lived there. Therefore it was named 'The Haunted House'. You should never go to that house. Otherwise, the house will eat you up."

I was scared imagining the visuals of the house being a monster and eating me. I rushed to my bed and hid under the blanket.

Those memories have now passed and I wonder how foolish I was as a child. 'How can a house eat a human?'

Now I have grown up. Let's explore 'Why the house is HAUNTED?'

I stepped inside the house which was pitch dark to make out anything. The windows were all sealed up so that not even a single ray of sunlight could enter. Then I heard a voice "Who's there? For what have you came to my house?"

I was scared a bit and with a trembling voice, I replied. "Hello there, I'm your neighbour. I just came to check upon you."

He said, "Oh! So the beautiful young lady is my neighbour! Pleased to meet you."

"Why is it so dark in here?"

"This is for protection. You know I'm allergic to sun rays."

"Oh! I see," I was speechless.

"Were you not afraid of coming here?"

"Afraid of what?" I questioned back.

"I am sure you must have heard rumors of this house being haunted."

"Yes I did, from my childhood."

"Then... also, you are brave enough to come."

"I believe them to be stories for kids so that they won't dare do any mischief."

"Very well then. What if it is true?"

"I am very sure you are not a ghost."

"Yes, you're right. I'm not a ghost... Because I am a vampire."

"You gotta be kidding me, you just want to scare the hell out of me."

"You aren't scared, are you? What do you think why the sun rays are blocked?"

He came closer to me as I felt his voice close to the ear. I felt like something was around my throat.

"You are allergic to it."

"Do you believe that? No wonder I like you a lot, but that's my reality. I am a vampire."

"I don't believe you... Vampires are a myth."

"You want me to make you believe?"

"Yes."

The dim lights turned on. He came out of the darkest corner and appeared in front of me... I was stunned... His complexion was pale yet his face was astonishing. His eye color was red but they were not bloody or horrific.

"Now do you believe that vampires are not a myth? They do co-exist with the humans."

I mumbled, "I do."

Then I fainted...!!!! I had a feeling of whispers in my ear. 'I Love You'

I opened my eyes that very instance & found myself in my bedroom on my bed.

Then dad entered and said, "You are awake sleepy head! Now pack your bags my work here is over... We are leaving, I was waiting for you to get up... You were deep in sleep like a baby when I arrived home. You would have been tired of a long journey, so I didn't wake you."

I pondered on what all happened. I was in the house next door... Yes, I know I was. But when did I reach my room? Was I dreaming?

I know everything is true. I talked to him, it was not a dream... Then I noticed there was something under my blanket. I removed the blanket and found a necklace box.

I opened the box and found a beautiful red pendant of the heart shape and a letter stating:

'Dear Love,

You are not dreaming... Yes, it's true you met me and talked to me. In centuries no one cared to know what lies inside this house as they were afraid, but you were different. You came across to know the well-being in the haunted house.

You have a very different charm, although your smell of blood was forcing me to turn you into a vampire and make you my queen for eternity, you charisma stopped me from doing so.

You know being a vampire might be a boon to live till eternity, but at the same time it's a huge curse of not dying and be thirsty for blood forever... and I can't curse my love of any kind.

You'll always be my queen (the human queen). As a token of love I am presenting you this heart pendant.

Love from,

Your Neighbor (Vampire Next Door).'

HALLOWEEN PARTY INVITATION TO VAMPIRE VILLA

It's the last week of the month of October... The festival of Halloween is about to arrive. Only a few days are left. The town was so excited.

Suddenly, the doorbell rings... I went to look who's at the door. When I opened it no one was there except the black envelope. It seemed to be an invitation card. I opened the card and read:

'Dear town people,

I, the Lord of VV house, which is popularly known as 'vampire villa' gladly invite you all to my house for the 'Halloween Party' at 11:00 p.m

From,

VV Lord'

I went out to the neighbours and saw that the whole town was invited to 'vampire villa'. Everyone had the same invitation card in the black envelope.

People were terrified & there was chaos, as nobody ever dared to go to vampire villa in the day time also. The vampire villa was located at uphill. It was visible from town but people never looked at it during the night because it was spooky.

The town people believed that the Lord of VV is Vampire. Therefore the villa is known as the 'VAMPIRE VILLA'.

People whispered that he 'VV' Lord (VAMPIRE) wants the whole town to be it's treated, so he is tricking them to Halloween party.

So they decided not to attend. But I made my mind to go uphill & find out the truth. So, I went to VAMPIRE VILLA... There was dead silence inside the house and it was creepy. I knocked on the door... It opened on its own, no one had attended the door.

I stepped inside... in the hall somebody was sitting on a sofa with the back facing my side. He said, "Hello Miss... I see you are all alone. Where are the others?"

"I don't know... I came to the party."

"Well then... I guess I have to be contained with you only..."

After that, the lights started flickering. My visuals got distraught. I felt heavy pain at the neck as if someone had bit me... I tried screaming but failed due to the pain and was getting dizzy because I was losing energy.

"You were my treat... Now let the party begin."

Slow violin started playing and the UU Lord started dancing with my half-life body. I was not in full sense but somewhat I was able to make out what was happening in the surrounding.

MY CHILDHOOD FRIEND – A VAMPIRE

I am Sarah. I lived in 'House No. 20, cross lane, at the North Street. I grew up in this town of COLD VALLEY. The house adjacent to mine was, empty for years... That house belonged to my childhood friend Victor.

The Victor family left the town when I was 10. In there is a tree which I and Victor planted in our childhood together, we named the tree Sah-vir (Sarah & Victor).

After 20 years, one car stopped in front of Victor's house, that was a luxury car. Two people stepped outside; one man and one lady.

The guy was a heartthrob. All the girls in town were just mesmerized by him... But he ignored all. As they were about to enter he turned and locked his eyes with me. We were lost in each other, then the lady with her snapped her finger in front of him then only he stopped gazing at me.

She signed him of getting inside the house. At the bottom of my heart, I felt some connection with this hunk, as if I knew this stranger. I thought 'Who can these people be?'

In the evening I went over to meet my new neighbours. I knocked on the door. The lady opened the door, she seemed to be a bit odd to me, the way she was checking me out was as if I was her meal & at an instant she attacks.

As she was about to step towards me the voice behind called 'Maria' and the lady turned... She said, "I guess today's.."

She was yet to complete her sentence again the same voice of that guy interrupted and said, "Maria... you are yet to settle your stuff. Let me take over the guest."

Maria: But.. (She tried to speak)

The Guy: You Heard Me.

Maria seemed displeased & was glaring at me, her behavior made me uncomfortable. She left to room.

The Guy: I am sorry about that Sarah... My sister is a bit haughty.

Me: It's ok, but how do you know my name..?

The Guy: I believe you don't recognize me... I see that Sah-vir has grown up to a beautiful tree from the sapling when I left the town.

Me: (excitedly) Victor... I just rushed & hugged him tightly.

He was uneasy. I thought did I cause a blunder in over-excitement. I stepped back & said sorry.

Victor: It's perfectly fine... I know we are meeting after years.

Me: Actually.

After few minutes...

Me: Victor... Maria...??

He guessed what was I curious about... as Victor was the only child then how is Maria his sister.

Victor: Maria is my cousin, my aunt's daughter.

Me: Oh I see.

Then Maria appeared and said, "Vic, I am thirsty... Why are you playing around? It's very tempting."

Victor: Hold up Maria, I am not playing around & you would do nothing.

Maria: (agitatedly) why not....? She is just a human.

I was really confused about their quarreling.

Victor: (enraged) Don't you dare hurt her.

Maria: As if I care...

And she marched towards me.

Victor shielding me grabbed Maria's throat with his fangs and said: Enough

Maria also with her fangs retaliating.

Only then I realized both Victor & Maria are vampires...

Victor choked Maria, Maria accepted her defeat... after that Victor released Maria and ordered her to leave.

Maria: (coughing) Vic...

Victor: Do as I say

Maria left... Victor realizing I am terrified of his horrific figure come to normal.

Victor: I am sorry for all of these, whatever happened tonight, pardon me for this.

Me: (still in shock)

Victor: Sarah...!!!

Me: You Are A Vampire.

Victor: Yes

Me: (stammering) Bbbb....ut... Hhhh...ooow..???

Victor: Remember 20 years ago when I left COLD VALLEY.

Me: Yes.

Victor narrating... (Flashback)

After leaving town we were staying with my aunt, she was a single mother with her only child Maria. Due to some emergency, my parents had to go out but met with an accident. They died... now all the responsibility was on my aunt. Aunt always has to go out in the dense forest for collecting wood.

She was also growing old for chores. then Me & Maria decided to go to the forest & collect wood. But we got lost since we were new to the forest. While wandering we reached one house and thought of taking shelter for a moment & ask directions to get out of the forest, as we entered the house.

The house we entered was the house of vampire... who then turned us.

Flashback ends.

Me: Then being a vampire why were you protecting me against Maria.. who herself is vampire, why you did not turn me?

Victor: Because I might be a vampire, but I am also your childhood friend... & friends don't eat their friends, do they...?

We hugged each other.

VAMPIRE - MY GUARDIAN ANGEL

I lived with my aunt KIARA, she was my caretaker as well. She has taken care of me since childhood. Aunt KIARA is not my blood-relation... yet she was my family, she was the only family I knew, she was my mother figure.

Aunt KIARA also loved me like her daughter. It was dinner time after finishing the meal... Aunt KIARA poured the red liquid into the glass, do you know what is it... No, it' not red wine...!!!

It's 'BLOOD'; yes aunt KIARA was drinking blood & I was not terrified because I knew her secret from my childhood only... That aunt KIARA is 'VAMPIRE'. When I was a newborn child... I was left in the woods to be the food of fierce animals, the hungry wolves were ready to tear my flesh, they jumped on me but something stopped them...

It was Aunt KIARA, she scared them away. Aunt KIARA was the most powerful vampiress with whom none dared to fight... every creature in the woods was aware of it.

The innocence of the baby turned the most powerful vampires to the MOTHER & From that day onward aunt KIARA was my protector.

That is how the VAMPIRE is my GUARDIAN ANGEL.